my life pages

A Companion to The Lotus and the Lily

JANET CONNER

STARTED _____ FINISHED_____

Conari Press

First published in 2013 by Conari Press, an imprint of
Red Wheel/Weiser, LLC
With offices at:
665 Third Street, Suite 400
San Francisco, CA 94107
www.redwheelweiser.com

ISBN: 978-1-57324-618-7

Library of Congress Cataloging-in-Publication Data available upon request

Cover design by Jim Warner
Cover photograph © dieKleinert / SuperStock
Interior by Nancy Condon
Typeset in Mrs Eaves and Gill Sans Std
Mandala graphics by Sandy Cromp, Sunshine Design Studio

The author gratefully acknowledges permission to quote from:

#11 from Tao Te Ching by Lao Tzu, A New English Version, with Foreword and Notes, by Stephen Mitchell. Translation © 1988 by Stephen Mitchell. Reprinted by permission of HarperCollins Publishers.

"Verse 27", from Tao Te Ching: The Definitive Edition by Lao Tzu, translated by Jonathan Star, © 2001 by Jonathan Star. Used by permission of Jeremy P. Tarcher, an imprint of Penguin Group (USA) Inc.

Printed in the United States of America
MAL

10 9 8 7 6 5 4 3 2 1

The paper used in this publication meets the minimum requirements of the American National Standard for Information Sciences—Permanence of Paper for Printed Library Materials Z39.48-1992 (R1997).

contents

Welcome from The Voice

Beloved,

    You hold in your hands an open container, a gentle space for our conversations about your life. What is your life? Have you considered this question? From where I sit—and I sit in you—your life is already beautiful. You move, and light shimmers. You breathe and I breathe. You touch; we feel. How can it be otherwise?

    Come, Beloved. Welcome to the mystery of you. If there be tears, we shall weep them. If there be songs, we will sing them. When puzzles come, we will giggle together at the wonder of it all. Do you feel the wind stirring your hair? The sun on your skin? The shiver of ice, the song of the crow, the breath of the baby? You are welcome.

    I know you. Come, Beloved, the season has come to know yourself.

The Voice

How to Use My Life Pages

I've been deep soul writing since 1997. I've written in every kind of journal imaginable from fast food napkins to oversized sketch pads. I've written in expensive art journals and bargain bin specials. I've written in my son's leftover school composition books, and once, just once, I wrote in a blue, suede beauty. I think I rubbed it more than I wrote in it. Now, as I create journal companions for my own books, I get to put the best of what I learned from the thousands of pages that have passed through my hands into a new kind of journal—and hand it to you.

My Life Pages is a companion to *The Lotus and The Lily*, but you do not have to be reading the book to benefit fully from this unusual journal. And it is unusual. It opens with a welcome from the Voice that came on my pages. I'm quite certain those words are for you. The pages are numbered, so you can easily return to conversations. I've included the Seven Steps to Get into Theta, so you can be certain you are soul writing, not journaling. There are four sets of Capture Pages where you can record wisdom you want to remember forever. In the back, there are images you can cut out for the center of your Intention Mandala. (Or just color them or rip them out and use them as bookmarks.) My closet is full of journals with a strip of masking tape on the cover noting the beginning and ending dates—effective, but not pretty. You have a little box on the title page. Ten years from now, you'll thank me.

But what really sets my journals apart are the quotes. As you write, you will stumble upon quotations from masters and mystics of all traditions on the left hand side, and snippets from *The Lotus and the Lily* on the right. When you come upon a quote, stop, read the words, and if they speak to you in some way, read them again, out loud perhaps. Taking a moment to digest wisdom this way moves ideas off the page and into your being, where they can feed you.

When I come upon ideas that feel important, I ask my Voice questions like: What does this mean? Is this true for me? What is this teaching me? Or, why am I uncomfortable with this? Questions activate the Voice, so I've added one or two to stimulate your own conversation. Of course, you don't have to use any of my questions. They're just a little soul writing gift from me.

Here's a quote from one of my favorite authors to get you excited about the journey ahead.

> Creation is always in the heave of growth and becoming and when a thing journeys towards its own perfection or fullness of life, it is also secretly journeying towards the divine likeness. . . . There is a wonderful urgency within things to realize the dream of their individual fulfillment; nothing is neutral, everything is on its way.
>
> —John O'Donohue, *Beauty*

Read this aloud. Read it again. This isn't just a lovely idea; this is real. It means you are in the heave of growth. You are becoming. You are journeying toward your own perfection. And it means that you, too, are on a secret journey into the truth about your own divine likeness. How thrilling. Do you feel a swell of urgency, a longing to fulfill who and what you came here to be? You are not neutral. Heavens, no. You are a soul. You are a wild, glorious, and hungry soul who came to play in these exciting, if often puzzling, fields of life. You are alive. And you are on your way.

May this journal serve your travels well.

Janet Conner

A Quick Review of the Seven Steps to Get into Theta

When we soul write, our speedy beta brainwaves slow down until we touch theta. Brain science indicates that we have access to breakthrough thinking and creativity in theta— exactly what we need to create a life of beauty and joy. There is an even deeper theta called mystical theta. How do you know you're in theta or mystical theta? Some soul writers feel tingling in their arm or hand. For others, the pen takes off, or their handwriting changes, or the pronouns shift. Over time, you will discover your own personal theta signature. You may not slip into theta every time you pick up a pen, but these seven steps will help you deepen your writing practice from journaling to writing down your soul.

1. Set your intention to exit conscious mind and access your extraordinary Voice. Do this with a few breaths, a thought, a prayer, by touching your third eye, visualizing light. There is no end to the ways you can set your intention. It takes just a moment, but don't leave this initial step out.

2. Address the Voice by name. If you don't have a private and personal name, simply write Dear Voice. Eventually a name will make itself known.

3. Write by hand. A lot of neurologically juicy things happen when you write by hand. You activate both sides of the brain, increase focus, find resolution, and remember what's important. As far as the brain is concerned, writing about something is a mini-rehearsal for doing it. No wonder soul writing is the ideal place to give birth to a beautiful life. All these good things happen because writing by hand utilizes vision, touch, and hearing simultaneously.

4. Activate all five senses. Smell is the most powerful sense you have. Activate it with candles, essential oils, fresh flowers, or by opening the window. For taste, keep a glass of water beside you when you write and slowly drink it when you finish, whispering aloud any wisdom or blessing that came through. (Read the full story of why we drink water in *Writing Down Your Soul*.)

5. Ask questions. Answers are a straight line from A to B. Once you reach an answer, you are finished, full, sated. Life, however, is not a straight line; it's a spiral, carving ever more deeply into the mystery with every turn. Ask big questions and watch what happens.

6. Write fast. Writing quickly catapults you out of conscious mind. This is a good thing because when the conscious mind is not operative, new information can flow to you from anywhere in the universe. To write quickly you must ignore all those things your English teachers cared about: spelling, grammar, punctuation, handwriting. The messier, the better.

7. Be grateful. You were heard. Don't forget to say thank you as you drink your water.

Theta in the Morning

As you awaken, your brainwaves drift naturally from the slow delta sleep waves through theta and into the faster waves. Everyone has access to a few rich theta-drenched moments, but most of us leap out of bed leaving the magic on the pillow. Here's how to maximize theta in the morning.

1. Put a notepad and open ballpoint pen next to the bed.

2. If you want specific guidance, ask a question as you are falling asleep.

3. If you are awakened in the night, roll over in the dark and write down what you hear. Put your pen below what you've written, whisper thank you, and go back to sleep.

4. When you wake in the morning, do not open your eyes, turn your head, or get up. Lie still. Dreams, ideas, and information will simply come to you.

5. When you finally get up, look at your night messages on the pad.

At first you may feel rather silly lying still in bed, but over time, you'll discover that massive amounts of creative solutions and ideas flow effortlessly to you in the morning. This is when I do my best "work."

¡ ?

paradox alerts

Only the paradox comes anywhere near to comprehending the fullness of life.

—Carl Jung, *Psychology and Alchemy*

The Lotus and The Lily is sprinkled with Paradox Alert sidebars. We are uncomfortable with paradox. How can two seemingly different things be simultaneously true? But paradox is the Divine's favorite language. When you stumble upon a paradox, stop, pay attention. Let it cook inside of you. Notice how it plays out on the page and in life. Wrestle with it, and as you do you will learn something about the mysteries of your own life. These four pages are set aside like a frame for your paradoxes. But please don't think recording them here means you understand them. On the contrary, the best ones become lifelong companions. Here's one of my companions: to be full, you must be empty.

¿ ¿

‽

¿¿

nourish statements

The soul needs an intense, full-bodied spiritual life as much as and in the same way that the body needs food.
—Thomas Moore, *Care of the Soul*

What feeds your soul? What words, prayers, thoughts, activities, or spiritual practices? How do you nourish your beautiful, abundant life? Each day in *The Lotus and The Lily* ends with a nourish statement that captures the essence of the spiritual food for that day. Whether you are reading the book or not, use these special pages to capture your personal food. Make a list. And return here often, especially when your soul gets hungry.

1.

2.

3.

4.

5.

6.

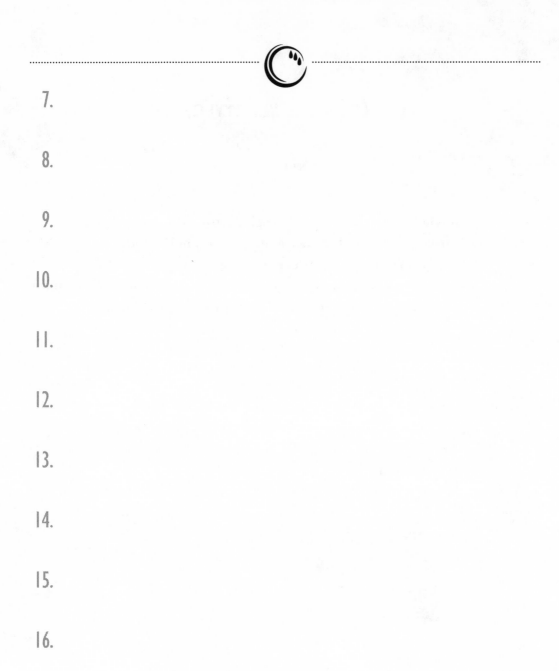

7.

8.

9.

10.

11.

12.

13.

14.

15.

16.

17.

18.

19.

20.

21.

22.

23.

24.

25.

26.

27.

28.

29.

30.

31.

32.

wisdom of my voice

They can be like a sun, words.

They can do for the heart

what light can

for a field.

—St John of the Cross, "They can be like a sun," translation by Daniel Ladinsky

A big frustration deep soul writers often express is not being able to easily find the beautiful wisdom and guidance that came through on their pages. Even the most stunning words can be swamped by the thousands of others that pour around them on the page. So, when something comes through that you wish to savor again, circle it, or mark it with a little star or check mark, and when you've finished writing, look back at what you've marked. If it calls to be "captured," post it here. By the time you fill this journal, you will have a rich compendium of your personal words of light.

You chose this human experience, and you came to live in beauty, not in pain—to consume life, not to be consumed by it.

Am I consuming life or being consumed by it?

If we fail to acquaint ourselves with soul, we will remain strangers in our own lives.

—John O'Donohue, Beauty

How am I a stranger in my own life?

You are here for life; and if you are here for life, life will be here for you.

—*Thich Nhat Hanh*, You Are Here

Am I fully present for my own life?

You are a soul. That means you are brimming with innate spiritual intelligence.

How am I using my spiritual intelligence?

Life will give you whatever experience is most helpful for the evolution of your consciousness. How do you know this is the experience you need? Because this is the experience you are having at this moment.

—*Eckhart Tolle*, A New Earth

What experience is life giving me at this moment?

You were born to create.
The creative powers of desire,
imagination, and intention were
built into you at the factory.

How have I been using my creative powers?

Vocatus atque non vocatus, Deus aderit.

Bidden or unbidden, God is present.

—Erasmus, carved over Jung's door and on his tomb

Do I bid the Divine to be with me?

Do I sense divine presence?

This is the secret of the mystical life; this is the secret of the spiritual life. It is all embodied in the one word consciously. Those who consciously know the truth are those who experience truth because truth is present, whether or not they know it.

—Joel Goldsmith, The Contemplative Life

What is my life telling me about my consciousness?

It's possible that the very thing you are wrestling with—and trying so hard to make go away—is exactly what you're here to unravel. Don't run away from your mysteries, run into them.

Am I willing to run into my mysteries?

Care of the soul is not solving the puzzle of life; quite the opposite, it is an appreciation of the paradoxical mysteries that blend light and darkness into the grandeur of what human life and culture can be.

—Thomas Moore, Care of the Soul

Am I learning to appreciate the mystery of my life or am I trying to solve it?

It's important to live life with the experience, and therefore the knowledge, of its mystery and of your own mystery. . . . [L]earn to recognize the positive values in what appear to be the negative moments and aspects of your life. The big question is whether you are going to be able to say a hearty yes to your adventure.

—Joseph Campbell

Can I say a hearty yes to my life's adventure—all of it?

You are an embodied soul. What your soul experiences, your body experiences. What your body experiences, your soul experiences. Treat your whole self with love and tenderness.

How do I treat myself?

> *Be a light unto yourself.*
> —The Buddha

How content am
I with myself?

There is no substitute for silence, because it is in silence that the soul speaks.

Do I relish silence or avoid it?

*The eye with which I see God is the
same eye with which God sees me.*

—*Meister Eckhart*

How do the Divine and I see one another?

*There is an uncanny symmetry between the inner and the outer world.
Each person is the sole inhabitant of their own inner world; no-one
else can get in there to configure how things are seen. Each of us is
responsible for how we see, and how we see determines what we see.*

—*John O'Donohue,* Beauty

How do I see? And what am I seeing as a result?

If you want a new life of abundance and joy, your first step is to prepare yourself for it. Give yourself the gift of preparation.

Do I value preparation?

I felt in need of a great pilgrimage
so I sat still for three
days

and God came
to me.
—Kabir, "A Great Pilgrimage," translation by Daniel Ladinsky

How do I invite Spirit?
Are there new ways I'd like to try?

When you enter into a creative endeavor with a clear image of the outcome, you are not entering into a creative endeavor. You are controlling it, or managing it, or wrestling it to the ground, but you are not allowing it and all its gifts to come to you.

Am I controlling or allowing?

Spirituality need not be grandiose in its ceremonials. Indeed, the soul might benefit most when its spiritual life is performed in the context it favors—ordinary daily vernacular life. But spirituality does demand attention, mindfulness, regularity, and devotion. It asks for some small measure of withdrawal from a word set up to ignore soul.

—Thomas Moore, Care of the Soul

How much attention do I give my soul and my spiritual life?

But as for you, when you pray, enter into your inner chamber and lock your door, and pray to your Father who is in secret, and your Father who sees in secret shall himself reward you openly.

—Jesus, Matthew 6:6, Holy Bible from the Ancient Eastern Text

How often do I stop and meet the Divine?

Everything begins with intention. Whether you are consciously aware of your intentions or not, every move you make is powered by a potent but invisible internal engine—your intentions, thoughts, feelings, and desires.

How do I use the power of intention?

> *We are so captivated by and entangled in our subjective consciousness that we have forgotten the age-old fact that God speaks chiefly through dreams and visions.*
>
> —*C. G. Jung,* Man And His Symbols

What are my dreams telling me?

> *[T]he way God speaks is elusive and often mysterious, for God's voice is the language of dreams and landscapes, of art and music, of dancing and poetry. It does not lend itself easily to a world conditioned to sound bites.*
>
> —*Christine Valters Paintner, PhD,* Lectio Divina

How is the Divine talking to me?
Am I listening?

You are not alone. You have never been alone. And you will never be alone. You are always and forever surrounded by divinely appointed guides.

Do I sense the presence of my guides?

No experience has been too unimportant, and the smallest event unfolds like a fate, and fate itself is like a wonderful, wide fabric in which every thread is guided by an infinitely tender hand and laid alongside another thread and is held and supported by a hundred others.

—Rainer Maria Rilke, Letters to a Young Poet, Letter 3

Can I see my life as a tapestry sewn by a beautiful hand?

You are your own shaman. You have direct and immediate access to Spirit.

How am I using, or not using, my mystical powers?

*Frequently, in a journey of the soul, the most precious
moments are the mistakes. They have brought you to a
place that you would otherwise have always avoided.*
                                    —John O'Donohue, Anam Cara

Where have my mistakes brought me?

*Soul enters life from below, through the cracks,
finding an opening into life at the points where
smooth functioning breaks down.*
                        —Thomas Moore, Care of the Soul

What are my cracks and how is my soul
bubbling up through them?

The best prayer, the most powerful prayer, is the one that rises from the wellspring of your soul.

How do I pray? Do I want to change the way I pray?

Faith does not rely on knowing anything with certainty.
It requires only the courage to accept that whatever
happens is for the highest good.

          —*Dan Millman*, The Journey of Socrates

Do I have the courage to view what is happening
as good even though it doesn't feel good?

Life is simple. Everything happens for you, not to you. Everything
happens at exactly the right moment, neither too soon nor too late. You
don't have to like it . . . it's just easier if you do.

          —*Byron Katie*, Loving What Is

Is my life more often simple and easy? Or difficult and hard?

Pay attention to the odd twists and little surprises of life. The soul takes nothing—nothing—for granted.

What have I been taking for granted?

Mature people are not either–or thinkers, but they bathe in the ocean of both–and.

—*Richard Rohr,* Falling Upward

Am I more of an either-or or both-and person?

True beauty can emerge at the most vigorous threshold where the oppositions in life confront and engage each other.

—*John O'Donohue,* Beauty

When opposites collide in my life, how do I respond?

There are gifts of wisdom and grace in the life you have already created. Before you consider what you want in the future, look back at your past as if you were gently picking up rocks and turning them over in your hand.

What do I see when I turn over the rocks of my life?

Worry is not concern which would motivate you to do everything possible in a situation. Worry is a useless mulling over of things we cannot change.
—Peace Pilgrim, Peace Pilgrim: Her Life And Work In Her Own Words

How much of my life is lost in worry?

There is nothing that wastes the body like worry, and one who has any faith in God should be ashamed to worry about anything whatsoever.
—Mahatma Gandhi

Am I worrying because I don't trust God?

That is why I am telling you not to worry about your life and what you are to eat, nor about your body and what you are to wear. Surely life is more than food, and the body more than clothing.
—Jesus, Matthew 6:25, New Jerusalem Bible

What am I worrying about? How can I stop?

Consider the possibility that nothing is happening to you. But many, many things are happening for you—for your wholeness, for your perfection, for your soul's evolution.

How is my life moving toward wholeness?

Nothing ever happened in the past that can prevent you from being present now; and if the past cannot prevent you from being present now, what power does it have?

—*Eckhart Tolle*, A New Earth

Am I living in the present or drifting back to old wounds and stories?

The best way to take care of the future is to take care of the present moment.

—*Thich Nhat Hanh*, Living Buddha, Living Christ

How am I nourishing my life right now—today, this very moment?

Every thought has magnetic power. Every feeling percolates out of us to find its match. But here's the problem: it's not just the pretty thoughts and feelings that have power.

What have I created?

To bless whatever there is, and for no other reason but simply because it is—that is our reason d'être; that is what we are made for as human beings.
—Brother David Steindl-Rast, Gratefulness, the Heart of Prayer

Can I bless what is, just because it is?

The seeds of every new beginning are present in the ashes of every ending.

What is ending and beginning right now?

You hold in your hand an invitation: to remember the transforming power of forgiveness and loving kindness. To remember that no matter where you are and what you face, within your heart peace is possible.

—Jack Kornfield

How shall I find my way to a peaceful heart?

Look at your past for a pattern
of waking and sleeping.
When you can clearly see
and recognize these two very
different conditions, you'll know
something big about yourself.

Am I more awake or more asleep?

Sometimes the best thing we can do is stop and let go. When we do this our breath naturally returns to a more normal rhythm, and we can clearly assess the situation in front of us. When life pierces our heart, sometimes we need to let the holes remain rather than fill them immediately.

—*Neil Douglas-Klotz,* The Sufi Book of Life

Am I willing to sit with my holes?

The gifts of our lives don't always come in foil-wrapped packages with golden bows. Sometimes the most important gifts come in the guise of defeat, rejection, loss, pain, or suffering.

What gifts have I received in crumpled packages?

I have often suspected that the most profound product of this world is tears. I don't mean that to be morbid. Rather, I mean that tears express that vulnerability in which we can endure having our heart broken and go right on loving. . . . That's our business down here. That's what we're here for.

—Cynthia Bourgeault, The Wisdom Jesus

How can I endure and go on loving?

Fill my heart with Love, that my every teardrop may become a star.

—Hazrat Inayat Khan

What needs to happen so that my tears stop hurting and become stars?

Say thank you for all the luscious things in your life and everyone who said yes. And say thank you for the sorrows, frustrations, dead ends, rejections, and all the people who said no.

Can I say thank you for both yes and no?

If there is someone who disturbs my peace of mind, I can escape by locking my door and sitting quietly alone. But I cannot do that with anger! Wherever I go, it is always there, Even though I have locked my room, the anger is still inside. Unless you adopt a certain method, there is no possibility of escape. Therefore, hatred or anger—and here I mean negative anger—is ultimately the real destroyer of my peace of mind and is therefore my true enemy.
—His Holiness the Dalai Lama, The Dalai Lama's Little Book of Wisdom

What is anger destroying in me?

If you circumambulated every holy shrine in the world ten times,

it would not get you to heaven as quick

as controlling your anger.
—Kabir, "Visiting Holy Shrines," translation by Daniel Ladinsky

Am I controlling anger or is anger controlling me?

Forgiveness is the most important, most essential, most freeing spiritual practice. But we don't want to do it. We've hung on to our wounds for so long that, in a strange way, they've become old friends.

What old friends am I ready to release?

Do not judge.
—Buddha, Dhammapada 4:7

Who do I judge?
How do I judge?
Why do I judge?

Judge not, that you may not be judged.
—Jesus, Matthew 7:1, Holy Bible from the Ancient Eastern Text

How is judging others affecting me?

An eye for an eye only ends up making the
whole world blind.
—Mahatma Gandhi,
The Story of My Experiments with Truth

Who do I want to see punished?
Can I let go of that desire?

Don't settle for the story as you've told it for years. That story just keeps you prisoner. Dig underneath the details of your old story to find a deeper story. Explore the hidden emotions and desires. Ask big questions until the deeper meaning of the story bubbles to the surface.

What's my deeper story teaching me?

By far the strongest poison to the human spirit is the inability to forgive oneself or another person.
—*Caroline Myss*, Anatomy of The Spirit

How much unforgiveness poison is in my system?
What's it doing to me?

Forgiveness improves family relationships, decreases depressive symptoms while enhancing empathy and life satisfaction, and it can heal a wounded romantic heart. Even the act of choosing to replace an unforgiving attitude with a forgiving one affects the peripheral and central nervous systems in ways that promote physical and psychological health.
—*Andrew Newberg, M.D.*, How God Changes Your Brain

Am I willing and ready to forgive?

There is really only one person who needs forgiving: you. Not the other guy—you. It's always you. The first wound, the greatest wound, and the hardest one to heal, is inside of you.

Can I forgive myself?

One of the most familiar of Jesus's teaching is "Love your neighbor as yourself." But we almost always hear that wrong. We hear "Love your neighbor as much as yourself". . . . If you listen closely to Jesus's teaching however, there is no "as much as" in there. It's just "Love your neighbor as yourself"—as a continuation of your very own being. It's a complete seeing that your neighbor is you.

—Cynthia Bourgeault, The Wisdom Jesus

If my neighbor is me and I am my neighbor, what has to change?

I am ready to stop clanging the bell of not enough. From this day forward, I am enough. I am more than enough.

Do I feel that I am enough—just as I am?

Asking for something from God does not mean talking God into it; it means an awakening of the gift within ourselves.

—*Richard Rohr*, The Naked Now

Am I trying to talk God into something?

The wonderful conductor, Sergiu Celibidache said, "We do not create music; we only create the conditions so that she can appear."

—*John O'Donohue*, Anam Cara

How can I create space for the "music" I want in my life?

Want freedom? Forgive.

Want a vibrant healthy body? Forgive.

Want to find your purpose? Forgive.

Want to feel joy? Forgive.

Want to love and be loved? Forgive.

Want a magical, vibrant, abundant life? Forgive!

Am I willing and ready to forgive?

We join spokes together in a wheel,
but it is the center hole
that makes the wagon move.

We shape clay into a pot,
but it is the emptiness inside
that holds whatever we want.

We hammer wood for a house,
but it is the inner space
that makes it livable.

We work with being,
but non-being is what we use.

—Lao Tzu, Tao Te Ching,
Verse 11, translation by Stephen Mitchell

What tools am I using to create my life?

The greatest of your spiritual powers may well be surrender.

Do I perceive surrender as a power or a problem?

> *[S]ince no man could ever love God too much,*
> *so also no man could ever trust him too much.*
> *Nothing that a man can do is so fitting as to have*
> *great trust in God. God never ceased to achieve*
> *great things through those who ever gained great*
> *confidence in him.*
>
> —*Meister Eckhart*

How much do I trust Spirit?

> *God prepares you for your spiritual*
> *journey, no matter how complicated,*
> *painful, or demanding it might become.*
> *For this reason, patience, trust, and faith*
> *must become constants for you . . . The*
> *divine will reveal its plan for you; you*
> *have to be open to receive it.*
>
> —*Caroline Myss,* Entering the Castle

Am I willing to wait in a state of trust for things to unfold?

Dear God, I'm choosing.
I'm closing the gap, filling it with forgiveness,
plugging the holes, and posting a sign:
Only love is spoken here.

Am I ready to speak only love?

You can have all good things—wealth, friends, kindness, love to give, and love to receive—once you have learned not to be blinded by them; learned to escape from disappointment and from repugnance at the idea that things are not as you want them to be.
—*Hazrat Inayat Khan, from* The Sufi Book of Life *by Neil Douglas-Klotz*

How blinded am I by the things I want?
How disappointed that I don't have them?

You don't actually want anything. You want the freedom the thing represents.

What do I really want?

There is a force within that gives you
life—Seek that.
In your body there lies a priceless jewel—
Seek that.
Oh, wandering Sufi, if you are in search
of the greatest treasure,
don't look outside. Look within, and
seek that.   —Rumi

What treasure am I seeking?
Where am I looking for it?

You are empirical evidence of the presence of God. You are a
demonstration of the manifestation of the divine. Your relationship to
spirit is beyond structure. Let go of the ties that would define and restrict
your heart and you will begin your divine discovery: you will soar.
—Mary Anne Radmacher, Lean Forward Into Your Life

What ties do I have to let go of to begin my divine discovery?

When I set a broader intention for a soul-satisfying outcome and leave the details of what, when, who, and how to Spirit, I end up receiving more than I can imagine.

Am I willing to stop telling Spirit what my life should look like?

> *God is a thousand times more eager*
> *to give than we are to receive.*
> —*Meister Eckhart*

How eager am I to receive?

> *God does not set a table for you or for me; god has*
> *set a table for this whole universe.*
> —*Joel Goldsmith,* The Contemplative Life

How can I see more of this great feast?

Now and forever, this is home. You belong here. You are one of its precious and powerful children—not a bad family to be a part of.

Do I feel like a precious and powerful member of the human family?

The greatest gift one can give is thanksgiving. In giving gifts, we give what we can spare, but in giving thanks we give ourselves. One who says, "Thank you" to another really says, "We belong together."

—*Brother David Steindl-Rast,* Gratefulness, the Heart of Prayer

What do I mean when I say thank you to a person or to God?

When you allow others to create for you, you are relinquishing your power.

When and to whom have I relinquished my power? What happened?

> *When you recover or discover something that nourishes your soul and brings joy, care enough about yourself to make room for it in your life.*
>
> —*Jean Shinoda Bolen*

Am I creating space in my life for what feeds me?

In the end, we all have the same purpose: We are all here to experience love, give love, be love. We are here to know joy, and light the way to joy for others. Really—that's it.

How am I spreading love and joy?

> *Those who are wise mold their lives in the same*
> *way carpenters shape wood, farmers water*
> *crops, and archers aim their arrows.*
> —*The Buddha,* Jesus, Buddha, Krishna & Lao Tzu:
> The Parallel Sayings, *translations by Richard Hooper*

How am I molding my life?
What am I becoming?

> *What a skilled man can do with a Hammer*
> *The advanced pilgrim can do with Thought.*
> *One builds their own seat in this world*
> *Using God—*
> *The only material, that is everywhere.*
> —*Hafiz,* "The Only Material," *translation by Daniel Ladinsky*

What kind of "seat" have I built?
What kind do I want to build?

The question isn't whether or not you have trust issues; it's how can you move through them. How can you reach that state where you know, and you know that you know, that you are always protected, always guided, always led?

What is my relationship with trust?

When conditions are sufficient there is a manifestation.

—*Thich Nhat Hanh,* You Are Here

How can I become a container in which
my beautiful life can grow?

*[W]hen we pursue a right relationship with the Universal One and
allow this relationship to realign our lives, we produce a condition of
receptivity in which anything we need to help us complete our purpose
in life will be supplied by the universe.*

—*Jesus,* Blessings of the Cosmos, *Neil Douglas-Klotz*

How can I bring myself into closer alignment with the One?

Time is the one gift you can give yourself. Give it. Honor yourself with the gift of a Soul Day. Create a space and time where your soul can speak at length. Give yourself the gift of being fully and completely present to yourself, your soul, and the Divine.

Am I hungry for the gift of time?

Control over the universe appears to be supernatural, but in truth such power is inherent and natural in everyone who attains "right remembrance" of his divine origin.

—Paramahansa Yogananda, Autobiography of A Yogi

What am I remembering about my divine origin?

They are like shy, young school kids—time and space, before the woman and the man who are intimate with God.

The realized soul can play with this universe the way a child can a ball.

—Theresa of Avila, from "The Grail," translation by Daniel Ladinsky

How intimate am I with my God?

When one lives through spiritual laws and divine nature, then the human experience becomes heaven on earth. That is the kingdom. It is bringing that which exists beyond the physical realm with the guidance of Christ-consciousness into the human being.

Am I experiencing a taste of heaven on earth?

Pouring yourself out makes the universe do the same.
—Neil Douglas-Klotz, Blessings of the Cosmos

What would pouring myself out look like?
Am I willing to do this?

Feel yourself being an opening through which energy flows from the
unmanifested Source of all life through you for the benefit of all.
—Eckhart Tolle, A New Earth

What divine gifts are flowing through me into the world?

Then I heard the voice of the Lord
saying: "Whom shall I send? Who
will be our messenger?" I answered
"Here I am, send me."
—Isaiah 6:8–9

Have I ever said, "Send me?"
Can I say it now?
What do I think will happen?

You can have anything you want—why, you can have things you don't even know you want—but not by focusing on them. Instead, put your undivided attention on your connection with the vibrant presence of the Divine within, and your life will change.

Where is my focus?

*Happiness is when what you think, what
you say, and what you do are in harmony.*
                                —*Mahatma Gandhi*

How aligned are my thoughts, words,
and actions?

*O you who have believed, why do
you say what you do not do?*
                        —*Qur'an, 61:2*

How big is the gap between
my talk and my walk?

Your soul knows the fertile environment it wants—needs—to create an abundant life. There is no other life quite like yours. No one else has your purpose, your gifts, your dreams, your vision. No one else can do what you are here to do.

How can I create my beautiful life?

When you speak with 100 percent of your being, your speech becomes mantra. In Buddhism, a mantra is a sacred formula that has the power to transform reality.

—Thich Nhat Hanh, You Are Here

How much of me is present when I pray? What parts of me are not?

Scripture says, "A short prayer pierces the heavens," and the Cloud of Unknowing explains that this is "because it is the prayer of a man's whole being." Virtually every religion has such a practice, from Islam and Judaism to Buddhism and Taoism, and it works because you are praying with all the "height, depth, length, and breadth" of your spirit.

—Caroline Myss, Entering the Castle

Do my prayers pierce the heavens?

There's big power
in a short prayer.

*What short prayer can
I say every day?*

Celebrate. You are always harvesting something. Celebrate your small harvest. You need not wait till your whole ship comes in.

What gifts, what small harvest, can I celebrate today?

The practice is to touch life deeply so that the Kingdom of God becomes a reality. This is not a matter of devotion. It is a matter of practice. The Kingdom of God is available here and now.
—Thich Nhat Hanh, Living Buddha, Living Christ

How can I shift "touching life deeply" from an idea to a living practice?

For behold, the kingdom of God is within you.
—Jesus, Luke 17:21, Holy Bible from the Ancient Eastern Text

Is the kingdom of God inside me?

Men talk about Bible miracles because there is no miracle in their lives.

Cease to gnaw that crust. There is ripe fruit over your head.

—Henry David Thoreau

What miracles are hanging ripe over my head?

Even the hills and fields are flowing,
so why do you feel you're all alone,
tears hugging you to yourself?
The world is a tree bowed down with fruit,
while you bend over stealing rotten apples.

—Rumi, The Sufi Book of Life, *translation by Neil Douglas-Klotz*

Do I usually look up for ripe fruit or down
for rotten apples?

What would you be doing right now if you knew that what you wanted was coming at the end of the week? Make a list and start doing those things today.

What would I be doing if I knew that what I wanted was almost here?

The secret of the spiritual life is to recognize consciously—consciously realize, accept, and declare—our oneness with our infinite, immortal, eternal Source, and accept the scriptural statement that all that the Father has is ours and that the place whereon we stand is holy ground.

—Joel Goldsmith, The Contemplative Life

How much of this "secret" am I consciously realizing and expressing?

The Father and I are one.

—Jesus, John 10:30, New Jerusalem Bible

What would my life look like if I knew I was one with the One?

One cannot create one's next moment out of frustration with the moment that is. Therefore, the moment that is before you is filled with beauty.

What beauty is in this moment?

*Remember that not getting what you want is
sometimes a wonderful stroke of luck.*
                    —His Holiness The Dalai Lama

What luck has come my way because
I didn't get what I wanted?
What is this teaching me about wanting?

You've heard the saying, "Dance like nobody's watching." Well, I say, pray like nobody's watching. But you might want to close the door.

How can I put my whole self into my prayers?

Giving and receiving are one
This is called,
>   *"The great wonder"*
>   *"The essential mystery"*
>   *"The very heart of all that is true"*
—Tao Te Ching, *from Verse 27, translation by Jonathan Star*

**Does my life look like I know that giving
and receiving are one?**

*To receive knowledge, you must first give, because the giving process
opens you up. . . . One cannot live unto oneself. Accept that and you
accept one of the great laws of the universe.*
—Sun Bear and Wabun, The Medicine Wheel

How can I be more open—giving and receiving more?

Refresh your spiritual life every day or as often as you can. Don't let weeks go by without feeding your soul. If you do, your land will begin to feel parched. If that should happen, don't be discouraged, just return and begin anew.

How refreshing is my spiritual life?

Joy does not simply happen to us. We have to choose joy and keep choosing it every day. . . . Joy is the experience of knowing that you are unconditionally loved and that nothing—sickness, failure, emotional distress, oppression, war, or even death—can take that love away.

—Henri Nouwen, The Heart of Henri Nouwen,
edited by Rebecca Laird and Michael J. Christensen

Am I choosing joy? Do I know that I am loved unconditionally—just as I am?

This is the day the Lord has made
let us rejoice and be glad in it.

—Psalms 118:24

How grateful am I for the gift of today?

When you arise in the morning,
give thanks for the morning light,
for your life and strength.
Give thanks for your food and the joy of living.
If you see no reason for giving thanks,
the fault lies in yourself.

—Tecumseh

What are my first thoughts in the morning?

Living your conditions means filtering all your choices and actions and decisions through the essence and meaning of those commitments. When you do that, decisions get easier. You know almost immediately what belongs in your world and what doesn't.

Am I fully living the conditions that nourish me?

In the end, just three things matter:
How well we have lived
How well we have loved
How well we have learned to let go
—Jack Kornfield

If I died today, how well would
I feel I have lived?

Life is the flash
of a firefly in the night.
It is the breath of a buffalo
in the winter.
It is the little shadow
which runs across the grass
and loses itself
in the sunset.
—Crowfoot, "Final Vision,"
American Indian Prayers & Poetry

How precious and sacred is my life
to me? To my loved ones? To God?

Not getting what you want may well be one of the most beautiful and mysterious aspects of creating a life in concert with the Divine.

How is not getting what I want a gift?

All shall be well, and all shall be well, and all manner of things shall be well.

—*Julian of Norwich,* Revelation of Love

Am I ready now to live every day knowing all shall be well?

When one creates a personal universe of joy, all are lifted. As your life becomes sweeter, you kiss the world.

How can I kiss the world today?

my conditions

When conditions are sufficient there is a manifestation.
—The Buddha

We all long to create a sweeter, more fulfilling life. And we can. The spiritual masters, Buddha and Jesus, unraveled the great paradox of prosperity for us long ago. They both said you create a beautiful life not by asking for anything, but by creating fertile conditions in which your beautiful life will naturally grow. Conditions are the actions, attitudes, or approaches you commit to live every day. Mine are: live in intention, say my prayers out loud, work in sacred space, do my holy work, focus only on what's coming in, and have a grateful heart. What are yours?

six symbols for the center
of your mandala

On the next six pages are several of the most popular images people select for the center of their mandala. You are welcome to cut them out. Write your conditions in, on, or around the symbol. Full instructions for how to make an Intention Mandala are in *The Lotus and the Lily.*

Butterfly

The cover symbol for *The Lotus and the Lily* and *My Life Pages* is a butterfly because the butterfly more than any other creature embodies and illustrates transformation. She begins as an egg, the seed of a beautiful idea, and evolves into a voracious caterpillar, the perfect metaphor for our hunger for life. But then, she goes deep within as a chrysalis and discovers who she really is. While she's in there, every cell of her body is transformed and she emerges as a new creature altogether, the glorious butterfly—surely the perfect image of your beautiful, abundant life.

Five-Pointed Star

Many people put a star or other symbol of light in the center of their mandala, representing the Light. If you have five conditions, this star might work well for you.

Six-Pointed Star

This star looks and feels very different from the five-pointed one.

Lily

A lot of people put a lotus or a lily at the center of their mandala. I have six conditions and use this lily. I write one condition on each of the petals. It's a very significant symbol for me, harkening back to Jesus's famous saying, "Consider the lilies...." The blank dot at the center is the center of the mandala—The One.

Lotus

Sandy Cromp, a truly gifted graphic artist, created this unique and very beautiful take on a lotus. The Buddha would approve, don't you think? I love to color this in layers.

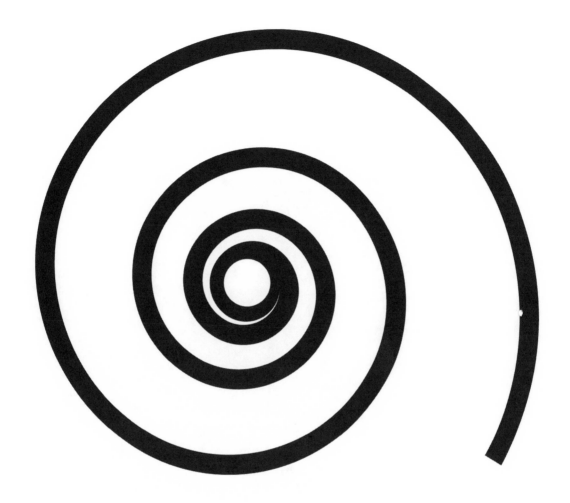

Spiral

As you have undoubtedly discovered in your deep soul writing, life is not a straight line, it's a spiral. Each day, we move deeper and deeper into its mysteries and yet, there's always more to discover. So it seemed fitting to offer a sacred spiral for your mandala. You can write your conditions in the spaces as they wind into the central circle which represents Source.

a blessing in parting

I wrote this blessing after a fire forced my spiritual community to hold services in the parking lot for a year. As I read it at the rededication, I realized I'd written much more than a blessing for a building; I'd written a blessing for life. (You can hear me read this at my website, *www.janetconner.com*.)

An Invitation from the Fire

This is where it all begins—the fire
Right here, right now

I didn't want the fire, I didn't choose fire
None of us wanted the fire
We would not have said: Yes, let's have a fire
Yes, let's force ourselves to change
Move outdoors, step aside from what we know, what we do, what we expect
Leave our comfy comfort, our little home, our lives as we know them
Why, yes, let's call upon fire to transform us

No, the fire had to come to us—invite us
Slither its way into our lives, up these walls, into this ceiling, and into this air
The fire had to welcome us—invite us—to the dance
Right this way, little children, to the Red Hot/Blue Cool brand new dance
The swing and sway of fire and peace, fire and peace, fire and peace

Fire is red hot
Fire changes things fast, in a flash, in a moment
What was, is not; what we knew, we can't be sure of
What we did, we can't do anymore; what we expected is gone, simply gone

Peace is blue cool
Peace changes things slowly, subtly, over time, as hearts melt a little, shift a little,
Move a little, blend a little, and then, a little more
Until I am in you and you are in me

This is where it begins—the fire
Right here and right now
Because I am the fire: I am hot red change; I choose to be red change
And I am the peace: I am that cool blue change; I choose to be blue change, too

That makes me a dancer, a Red Hot/Blue Cool dancer
I move fast, twirling and spinning in the fire power of God
And I turn slowly, bending softly in the peaceful strength of God
I am a dancer
The fire invited me to this dance
And I accept
From this time and this place on, I dance in the power and peace of God

about the author

SUNSHINE DESIGN STUDIO

Janet Conner is a vibrant writer, speaker, and teacher. She is the author of *Writing Down Your Soul* and its companion journal, *My Soul Pages*, as well as *The Lotus and the Lily*, from which this book is inspired. Her work has been featured in national media including Martha Stewart's Whole Living, Daily Word, DailyOm, Beliefnet.com, and more. Janet speaks nationally at conferences, churches, book events, and retreats and teaches a series of online courses to students worldwide. She lives in Ozona, Florida. Visit her at *www.janetconner.com*.

to our readers

Conari Press, an imprint of Red Wheel/Weiser, publishes books on topics ranging from spirituality, personal growth, and relationships to women's issues, parenting, and social issues. Our mission is to publish quality books that will make a difference in people's lives—how we feel about ourselves and how we relate to one another. We value integrity, compassion, and receptivity, both in the books we publish and in the way we do business.

Our readers are our most important resource, and we appreciate your input, suggestions, and ideas about what you would like to see published.

Visit our website at *www.redwheelweiser.com* to learn about our upcoming books and free downloads, and be sure to go to *www.redwheelweiser.com/newsletter/* to sign up for newsletters and exclusive offers.

You can also contact us at *info@redwheelweiser.com*.

Conari Press

an imprint of Red Wheel/Weiser, llc

665 Third Street, Suite 400

San Francisco, CA 94107